## Start TO Finish
*Second Series*

# FROM Cocoa Bean TO Chocolate

ROBIN NELSON

LERNER PUBLICATIONS › Minneapolis

Lerner Publications Company
A division of Lerner Publishing Group, Inc.
241 First Avenue North
Minneapolis, MN 55401 USA

For reading levels and more information, look up this title at www.lernerbooks.com.

Main body text set in Arta Std Book 20/26.
Typeface provided by International Typeface Corp.

**Photo Acknowledgments**
The images in this book are used with the permission of: © Biosphoto/Michel Gunther, pp. 1, 5; © Todd Strand/Independent Picture Service, pp. 3, 23; © Biosphoto/Antoine Lorgnier, p. 7; © Christopher Pillitz/The Image Bank/Getty Images, p. 9; © Richard T. Nowitz/CORBIS, p. 11; © Royalty-Free/CORBIS, p. 13; © Julian Brooks/Alamy, p. 15; © James L. Standfield/National Geographic/Getty Images, p. 17; © Frank Croes/Bon Appetit/Alamy, p. 19; © Gianluca Colla/Bloomberg via Getty Images, p. 21.

Front cover: © Alena Brozova/Dreamstime.com.

Library of Congress Cataloging-in-Publication Data

Nelson, Robin, 1971–
    From cocoa bean to chocolate / by Robin Nelson.
        p.   cm. — (Start to finish, second series. food)
    Includes index.
    ISBN 978–0–7613–6560–0 (lib. bdg. : alk. paper)
    ISBN 978–1–4677–0107–5 (EB pdf)
    1. Confectionery—Juvenile literature.
2. Chocolate—Juvenile literature. 3. Cacao beans—Juvenile literature. I. Title.
TX792.N454 2013
664'.5—dc23                    2011036404

Manufactured in the United States of America
9 - 44231 - 11608 - 5/10/2018

# TABLE OF Contents

# I love chocolate!

## How is it made?

## Cocoa beans **grow.**

A farmer plants many cocoa trees.
Hard **pods** grow on each tree. Inside
each pod are seeds called cocoa beans.

## Workers open the pods.

The pods grow for many months. Workers cut the pods from the trees. The workers open the pods with a large knife. There are twenty to fifty cocoa beans inside each pod.

## The sun dries the beans.

The cocoa beans are taken out of the pods.
Then they are left in the sun to dry for many
days.  The dry beans are put into large sacks.

**A train takes the beans to a factory.**

A train takes the sacks of cocoa beans to a chocolate factory. A factory is a place where things are made.

## The beans are roasted.

The beans are cleaned in the chocolate factory. Then the beans are roasted. Roasting the beans cooks them. It is easier to take shells off beans that have been roasted.

## Machines mash the beans.

The shells are taken off the beans.
Then the beans are mashed.
Mashing the beans turns them into a
very soft paste called **cocoa butter**.

## The chocolate is mixed.

Milk and sugar are added to the cocoa butter to make chocolate. The chocolate is heated and mixed for several days. Mixing makes the chocolate smooth and creamy.

## The chocolate is poured.

The chocolate is poured into **molds**.
Molds are containers that are used to
shape things.  The chocolate is cooled
in the molds.  It becomes hard.

## The chocolate is wrapped.

The chocolate is taken out of the molds. Machines wrap the chocolate. Trucks take the wrapped chocolate to stores to be sold.

## I eat my favorite treat!

How many chocolate treats can you name? All the chocolate in them started as cocoa beans!

## Glossary

**cocoa beans (KOH-koh BEENZ):** seeds of a cocoa tree

**cocoa butter (KOH-koh BUH-tuhr):** a soft paste made from mashed cocoa beans

**factory (FAK-tuh-ree):** a building where things are made

**molds (MOHLDZ):** containers used to shape chocolate

**pods (PAHDZ):** fruits of a cocoa tree

## Index

LERNER e SOURCE

Expand learning beyond the printed book. Download free, complementary educational resources for this book from our website, www.lernerresource.com.